My Love,

Here's to one of our ~~[illegible]~~ of expressing how we feel about eachother.

Kissing is one of the most sensitive communications we have.

Some of my favorite time spent with you is in kissing.

Many hugs & kisses,

Richard

kissing

Photographs of the wonderful act of kissing

Introduction by **Eve Babitz**

Edited by
Marla Hamburg Kennedy & Susan Martin

Graystone Books, Marina del Rey, 1995

This catalog constitutes a selection of images
from the traveling exhibiton *Kissing* curated
by Marla Hamburg Kennedy of the
G. Ray Hawkins Gallery, Santa Monica, California

Cover: detail, "Paris Couple" by Frank Horvat
Book Design by Marika van Adelsberg

Copyright 1995 by Graystone Books

Seven Minutes in Heaven copyright 1995 by Eve Babitz

All photographs are copyrighted
to the photographers or
Estates of the photographers

Published by Graystone Books
520 Washington Boulevard, Suite 509
Marina del Rey, California 90292.
Telephone: 310 577 7683

Distributed by D.A.P.
636 Broadway
New York, NY 10012
Telephone: 800 338-BOOK
Fax: 212 673 2887

Printed and bound by Palace Press, Hong Kong

ISBN 0-9630570-4-9

ACKNOWLEDGEMENTS

The editors would like to gratefully acknowledge and thank Hiro Ikeda of H2O Company, Ltd., Yosuo Konishi, Keiko Murayama, Izumi Tsuboi, and especially Kenji Okuhira also of H2O; Ichiro Shimizu of Mitsukoshi, Ltd; G. Ray and Susan Hawkins, Susan Lee Tompkins, Elaine Hanneman and Stephen Pogostin of the G. Ray Hawkins Gallery; Steven Hamburg, Katherine Kennedy, Soca, Andre, and Eartha; Maureen Lambray and Tom Carney; Susan Becker; and especially all the photographers whose artistry contributed to making the *Kissing* show a success.

Kissing

Of all the subjects that have attracted photographers since photography began, few can match the emotional and cultural richness of kissing. The kiss: human contact in one of its purest, most incandescent forms, the ultimate token of love and affection, romance, greetings and farewells.

The kiss is an expressive vehicle for love, lust, happiness, reverence, grief – the full palette of human emotions. Yet, captured on film, the kiss conveys more than emotional meaning; it conveys historical and cultural meaning as well. So that when you gaze upon *Kissing*, you understand something about the human participants and the world they inhabit.

Virtually every important photographer has brought his or her vision to bear on the kiss. This collection brings together the very best of these photographs into a single source. Included are well-known images like Robert Doisneau's *Kiss by the Hotel de Ville*, which, in its romantic intensity, has become a bona fide cultural icon, the ultimate romantic picture that provokes that intoxicating feeling that only this intimate gesture can call forth. Included are photographs of kisses that cross nations, cultures and species: of love, family, ritual, social graces. *Kissing* contains ironic kisses, tender and bittersweet kisses, lustful kisses, high society's "air kisses," and the list goes on.

While the wide ranging photographs in this collection share a common subject, each one reflects the distinctive sensibilities of the respective artists. For while these images tell us much about the subjects and the world they inhabit, they end up telling us most of all about the human being on the other side of the lens. Whether it be kissing between people or animals, on the streets of New York City, on the banks of the Seine or under the Coney Island boardwalk, on the movie screen or at the zoo, the kiss transfixes our imagination and continues to delight, enchant, and perhaps even heal us.

To all who celebrate the kiss, the photograph, and the human heart, this *Kissing* catalog is dedicated.

Marla Hamburg Kennedy & Susan Martin

by Eve Babitz

When I was growing up we girls spent every waking moment trying to be more kissable. Every one of our assets that could be more appealing was exploited: our curly hair, our long eyelashes, our scent, our toothpaste, the way we talked – all to become adorable enough for boys to want to kiss us when we played *Spin the Bottle* and its more sophisticated cousin, *Seven Minutes in Heaven.*

You can get pretty disorganized kissing for seven minutes in a closet, but when I was twelve years old, we combined the two games so that when the bottle landed on a boy, you not only got to kiss him but also got to spend seven minutes with him in a closet – in other words "heaven." Or maybe this was just wishful thinking, a childish myth.

I can't remember if anyone ever really lasted the full seven minutes – parents and chaperones being the clever killjoys they were – but this was the fantasy we girls had: the bottle would land on the cutest boy (in those days, his name was Doug) and we'd get to kiss forever.

When I was in junior high school, my favorite reading matter was love comics – pre-Harlequin romance comic books which were all about women wishing they could kiss someone but were unable to do so until the last frame. Boys read adventure comics, crime stories, western trash. And when boys went to see a pirate movie with Errol Flynn and he kissed Maureen O'Hara at the end, they would squirm with nauseated revulsion and hide their eyes in the same way girls did when people were gruesomely killed.

Fortunately, this boy-stage didn't last forever.

It is almost as though kissing were invented by Hollywood as the only sensible ending to love stories – the golden moment when "happily ever after" was supposed to begin. I don't think boys would have, of their own volition, kissed girls were it not for the lessons they eventually learned from the silver screen. At best, in pre-Hollywood times, if people kissed it was in illustrations of a gallant knight kissing her ladyship's gloved hand, or in hearsay from the Bible like "So she caught him, and kissed him, and with an impudent face said unto him . . ."

Kissing involves all of your senses: sight, because you wouldn't want to kiss anyone not striking you as adorable enough to touch your lips; sound, because once a kiss starts, moans ensue and you hope it's inspirational; smell, though of course who knows what to make of the current testings on men that reveal what turns them on most is the smell of pumpkin pie; touch, because touching is why we kiss someone at all; and taste, of course.

In more ways than one, Taste is everything in kissing.

But there is one sense you don't need to worry about in kissing, the stuff mothers used to call "sense enough to come in out of the rain." This is the kind of good "sound" sense that you need to have in your friends, but it's not what you need in a lover. People who kiss you can get away with a lot, especially if you want to kiss them again. A lover who's been mean to you can stop you from leaving with a kiss if feeling you might never kiss him again makes you miserable.

When I was in junior high there was a boy all the girls were crazy about, Shaggy. He had the blackest hair, long enough to fall over his eyes and, in the hot sun, he smelled of Brillcream, a scent that ever since has hit me as an aphrodisiac. For almost a week of afternoons we would sit out on the cement steps that surrounded the cafeteria reading Mad Magazine. We would laugh at the same things and then he'd walk me to class and kiss me – both of us aflame with burning desire.

One Friday night Shaggy dropped by my house in a car with a bashed-in windshield – not a good sign, since anyway he was only fourteen and way too young to drive.

"We can't go in that car," I said. "We'll get busted." But he was fast and he wanted more than mere kissing. Suddenly one day he dumped me for this hot tomato named Julie with very impudent red lips. I didn't see him much after that, but the truth was that if I could have done more than kiss him to keep him kissing only me, I would have. It was only later I discovered that some guys will leave you for hotter tomatoes no matter how far you go. Love being the unfair thing it is.

Later, in high school, I knew another boy who had the lips all the girls wanted to kiss. We used to dream about kissing him all day long, just as all the boys in school used to wonder what it would be like to kiss this girl named Cami, a cream puff in a tight skirt and powder blue sweater to match her eyes. One rainy day during lunch, those two kissed each other in front of the whole student body and we all went limp. Time stood still for all of us – the moment more hot and steamy (and more innocent) – than sex could ever be.

I love when men kiss women's hands. When I was growing up, men who kissed women's hands were like men who could slow dance great – prizes above rubies. In Europe, everyone seems glad to do this, but in America the only man who ever kissed my hand anywhere near beautifully enough was an actor I ran into in a restaurant, a big flirt who had just come back from far away and nothing ever came of it.

Kissing, if it's done on both cheeks, is comraderie; if on one cheek, is coy; but in the middle, it could go anywhere – uphill to heaven or downhill to hellish squalor. When you kiss someone you just don't know where you'll wind up.

If we look at photographs of people kissing, it seems almost as though photographs are kisses, too. Paintings might be a total commitment, like making love, but photographs are a fleeting moment, "a kiss," a possibility, a flirtation, a glimpse across a crowded room. The great thing about a kiss is its potential, its possibilities, its mainline to commitment, its "what it can become." Like having a child, once you kiss a certain person, your life can change forever.

Looking at photographs of people kissing, we are like voyeurs. We always hope that in the wonderful act of kissing passion will simply take over. Which is how we wish it to be for Rhett and Scarlett and all the stars who kiss in movies. We hope that even though it's their job and they're only actors and they're surrounded by film crews, we **hope** when they kiss, that the kiss will get out of hand and take over and turn into a passionate love affair.

When I was in my early twenties, I came across a great book of Jacques-Henri Lartigue photographs with an elegant gold cover. In this book were pictures of his beautiful girlfriend in her incredible svelte stylishness and one could see that if there was going to be anything wonderful about the times we live in, it was going to be between people we love and photographs we take or they take or find of them which symbolize to us what love is, what touched us as the epitome of marvelousness: the thrill of the kiss we remember in the rain long, long ago.

I know, of course, that there are many other kinds of kisses besides stylish kisses. Teen lust kisses, kisses that bring comfort and joy and make life worth living, kisses of life and death and close calls, kisses of spontaneous victory, tribute, and relief. Family kisses, animal kisses and kisses of everyday habit which have nothing to do with *Seven Minutes in Heaven*. But to me, the kisses I want to remember, the ones in which the world turned to mush, could never show up in a photograph — even if one could have been taken in a pitch dark closet.

The last man who kissed me seriously was way too young for me and beautiful enough to be a lot of trouble. His shoulders were like angel's wings and his eyes like turquoise pools. He took me for a ride on his BMW motorcycle and when he said good bye, he kissed my cheek. Unlike most other men's kisses, this one landed straight in my dreams. . . .

But, I can't be dreaming about him — it would end in complete disorganization of my senses, like memories of *Spin the Bottle* — a game that could start here on earth and end up in heaven.

©ANNIE LEIBOVITZ.   Courtesy of DANZIGER GALLERY, NEW YORK

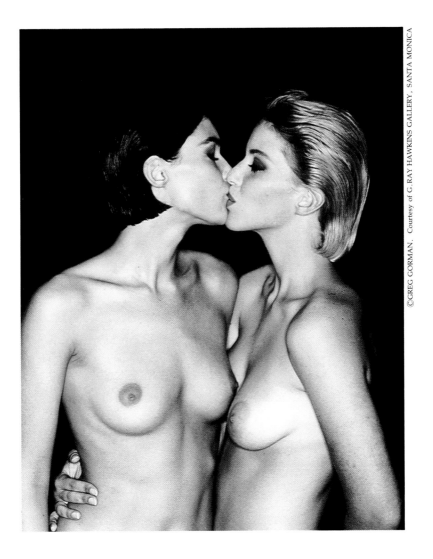

©PATRICK NAGATANI. Courtesy of G.RAY HAWKINS GALLERY, SANTA MONICA

© FRANK HORVAT / Courtesy of G. RAY HAWKINS GALLERY, SANTA MONICA & PETER HALPERT, NYC

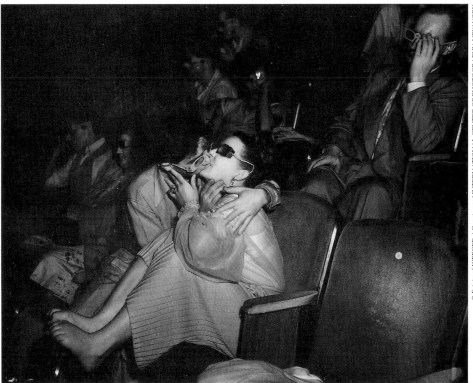

MANDY VAHABZADEH. Courtesy of G. RAY HAWKINS GALLERY, SANTA MONICA

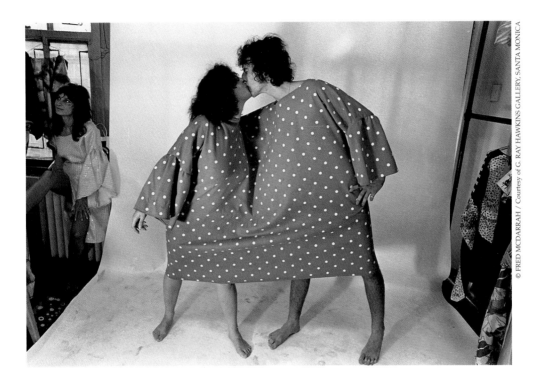

PHOTOGRAPHERS: EXHIBITION CHECKLIST

PHOTOGRAPHERS: EXHIBITION CHECKLIST

Lucien Aigner
Richard Avedon
James Balog
Tom Bianchi
Dianne Blell
Ken Browar
Horace Bristol
Larry Bump
Renee Burri
Debbie Fleming Caffery
Julia Margaret Cameron
Keith Carter
Henri Cartier-Bresson
Lucien Clergue
Alwyn Coates
Bruce Cratsley
George Daniell
Judy Dater
Henri Dauman
Bruce Davidson
Pamela Davis
Robert Doisneau
Eugene Druet
Arthur Elgort
Glen Erler
Eliott Erwitt
Dan Fauci
James Fee
Nat Fein
Larry Fink
John Flattau
Gary Franklin
Ed Freeman
Anthony Friedkin
Paul Fusco
Joe Gantz
Ralph Gibson
Nina Glaser
Nan Goldin
Greg Gorman
Allan Grant
Paul Greenberg
Milton Greene
Sid Grossman

Ernst Haas
Gregory Heisler
Karen Hirshan
Dennis Hopper
Frank Horvat
Eikoh Hosoe
George Hurrell
Bill Jacobson
Richard Kalvar
Andre Kertesz
E.F. Kitchen
Karen Knauer
Lewis Koch
Valeri Krupsky
Eddie Kuligowski
Maureen Lambray
Marcus Leatherdale
Annie Liebovitz
Arthur Leipzig
Leon Levinstein
Helen Levitt
O. Winston Link
Blake Little
Jim Long
Bret Lopez
Herb Lotz
Roxanne Lowit
Danny Lyon
Proshat Mahjoubie
Christopher Makos
Mary Ellen Mark
Bruce McBroom
Fred McDarrah
James McLoughlin
Sheila Metzner
Pedro Meyer
Marco Micheletti
Tom Millea
Ken Miller
Andrea Modica
Inge Morath
Joan Moss
Tom Mulvee
Joan Myers

Patrick Nagatani
Graham Nash
Genevieve Naylor
Helmut Newton
Nicholas Nixon
Ken O'Brien
Jean Pagliuso
Julia Parker
Georgy Petrusov
Laura Pettibone
Sylvia Plachy
Marc Riboud
Mary Robert
Matthew Rolston
Richard Ross
Andre Roy
Jan Saudek
Rocky Schenck
Jeffrey Schwarz
Sam Shaw
Larry Silver
Peggy Sirota
W. Eugene Smith
Louis Stettner
Rosalind Solomon
Dennis Stock
Lou Stoumen
Sherry Suris
Suzanne Tenner
Edmund Teske
Mikhail Trakhman
Mandy Vahabzadeh
James Van Der Zee
Sal Veder
Trevor Watson
Weegee
Jerry Weiss
Sabine Weiss
Hywel Williams
Bob Willoughby
Garry Winogrand
Pat York
Firooz Zahedi